Maggie and Barney and the Allergic Photographer

(It really happened!)

Other books by Marci Kladnik

Maggie Adopts a Kitten (It really happened!)

Look for these Maggie stories coming soon. They really happened!

Maggie Gets Into Trouble

Maggie and the Long Shadows

Maggie and the Magic Window Seat

Maggie's Special Animal Friends

Maggie and the Smelly Stuff

Maggie and Barney and the Allergic Photographer

(It really happened!)

Marci Kladnik

Illustrated by Stephanie Piro

Maggie and Barney and the Allergic Photographer (It really happened!)

Text copyright © 2020 by Marci Kladnik
Illustrations copyright © 2020 by Stephanie Piro

All rights reserved. No part of this publication may be reproduced or transmitted in any form or by any means, electronic or mechanical, including photocopy, recording, or any information storage and retrieval system, without permission in writing from the publisher, except by a reviewer quoting short passages.

Requests for permission to make copies of any part of this work should be mailed to the following address:

Mary Kladnik
PO Box 592
Los Alamos, CA 93440-0592

ISBN: 978-1-7345516-2-4 (hardcover)
ISBN: 978-1-7345516-3-1 (paperback)

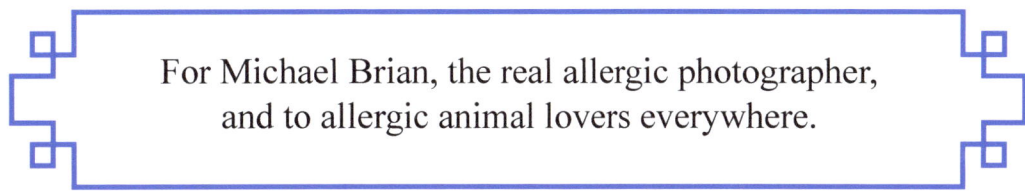

For Michael Brian, the real allergic photographer,
and to allergic animal lovers everywhere.

"A happy family of human, cats, and dog invite a photographer into their home to take pictures – but he can't stop sneezing. This charming tale and its joyful artwork show readers how delightful stories can be that "really happened!"

        Lonnie Hull DuPont, author of *Kit Kat & Lucy: The Country Cats Who Changed a City Girl's World*

"Funny, sweet, endearing. I'll definitely send a copy when my niece is born.

        Dusty Rainbolt, author of *Kittens for Dummies*

"Marci Kladnik expertly and delightfully captures the genuine friendship between a dog and a cat in her latest book, Maggie & Barney and The Allergic Photographer. This is a must-read for all ages!"

        Arden Moore, author of *A Kid's Guide to Cats* and host of the Oh Behave Show on Pet Life Radio.

Maggie was a Scottish terrier. From the very beginning, she was different. It wasn't because her right ear didn't stand up the way a Scottie's ears are supposed to. It wasn't because she liked to eat snails. It was because she liked cats, especially Barney.

Maggie and Barney lived with a nice lady named Marci in a large pink and white house in a tiny town. Three other cats lived with them. They are not part of this story except for the important fact that there were a lot of cats in the house.

Maggie's job was to protect their home while Marci's job was to rescue kittens born outside under bushes. She brought the kittens home to tame them so they could be adopted. Barney was one of those very wild little kittens when Marci brought him home.

There was a magical moment when the frightened kitten suddenly chose Maggie to be his new mom. Marci wrote a book about Maggie and Barney and word spread about that special moment.

SUDDENLY MAGGIE AND BARNEY WERE FAMOUS!

One day in early summer Marci's telephone rang. It was a woman calling from an important magazine. She told Marci they wanted to print the story about Maggie and Barney in their magazine! They would send a special photographer out in two weeks to take pictures of Maggie, Barney, and Marci.

WOW! THEY WERE GOING TO BE IN A BIG MAGAZINE!

There was a **LOT** to do before the photographer came!

The house had to be cleaned and so did the yard.

Maggie was very shaggy and didn't look like a proper Scottie, so she had to have a haircut. It would have to be a very special haircut, something only a groomer could do. Of course she'd also have to have a bath because her usually shiny black coat was pretty dirty from rolling on the grass and digging in the dirt in the backyard.

Maggie was always nervous when it was bath time because she was a little afraid of water. She was frightened because when she was a puppy, she had fallen into a duck pond and almost drowned.

Marci always bathed Maggie in the shower instead of a tub. Maggie still shivered in fear when the water was turned on, even though it was nice and warm and not cold, dark, and deep like that duck pond was!

Barney didn't have to have a bath because he always washed himself with his tongue like all cats do. He was a big boy, now, and didn't need help from Mommy Maggie to lick him clean after he ate. He didn't have to have a haircut, either, because his soft gray and white coat was always short and neat.

At last it was the **BIG DAY!** The house was clean, the yard was picked up, Maggie was clean and had a spiffy haircut. Barney and Marci were ready, too.

In the middle of the morning, the photographer and his assistant arrived. Maggie and Barney were taking their after breakfast naps together up on the window seat overlooking the neighborhood. When the car pulled into the driveway, Maggie woke up and started barking. Her job was to warn Marci when someone came to the house. When Maggie barked, Barney and the three other cats ran and hid under the bed.

The photographer's name was Michael, and his nice assistant's name was Shawna. They brought so many cameras and so much other equipment that they had to make many trips back and forth from the car to the house to bring it all inside. Maggie watched very carefully to be sure they didn't drop anything.

At last everything was in the house and Michael, Shawna, and Marci sat down to talk about what was going to happen that day.

Suddenly, Michael **SNEEZED**.

He **SNEEZED** again, and then a **THIRD** time and rubbed his eyes!

"Excuse be," Michael said. *"May I hab a tissue, please?"* He sounded a bit like he had a stuffy nose.

Marci handed him a box of tissues and Michael blew his nose loudly.

"Thag you bery buch," he said, rubbing his eyes again which by now were getting a bit red and puffy.

"How bany cats do you hab?" Michael asked.

"Four," replied Marci

"Oh dear," said Michael as he sneezed again and rubbed his eyes. *"Baybe we'd better go outside."*

OH NO, MICHAEL WAS ALLERGIC TO CATS!!

With so many cats in the house, how was Michael going to take Barney's picture?

Marci, Michael, Shawna, and Maggie all moved outside to the pink and white gazebo to continue talking. Barney stayed inside so Michael wouldn't keep sneezing and having to rub his eyes and blow his nose.

Outside in the fresh air, Michael felt much better, so it was decided that was where most of the picture-taking was going to happen. Barney would stay inside until it was his turn to be photographed.

Michael followed Maggie around the yard taking pictures of her near the flowers and in the gazebo swing with Marci. He took more pictures of them on the front porch. Maggie loved all the attention but especially all the treats she was getting for being good.

At last it was Barney's turn. Marci brought the cat outside and Michael took pictures of Barney hiding in the plants and relaxing in the sun. Michael stayed away from Barney, though, so he wouldn't sneeze. He had a special long camera lens that let him stay far away and still take pictures.

While Michael was taking pictures of Barney, Shawna and Marci set up a small table on the grass with a big white sheet hung up behind it. This was going to be a stage where Maggie and Barney would take turns having more pictures taken.

Maggie's turn was first because she was the star and also because she didn't make Michael sneeze.

Marci picked the dog up and put her on the table and told her to sit. When Maggie sat, Marci gave her a cookie for being good. Maggie liked that and waited for Marci to tell her to do something else so she could have another treat.

Michael took a lot of pictures of Maggie and then asked Marci if Maggie could stand on two legs.

Of course she could!

Marci held a cookie high above Maggie's head. Maggie stood up on her hind legs and stretched her neck uuup...and...uuuuup for the treat.

"GOOD GIRL!" said Marci, and gave Maggie her cookie.

Maggie had to do this **FIVE TIMES** before Michael got the perfect picture. The five cookies she earned made Maggie very happy.

When Michael had taken enough photos of Maggie, it was Barney's turn again. Maggie was glad because she needed a nap. She hadn't had one since morning and it was now the middle of the afternoon, so she trotted off to lie on the grass in the shade while Marci went to pick Barney up from where he was napping in the sun.

Barney was nervous about Michael and his camera. Barney didn't like being on the table, so Marci had to hold his back end while Michael took pictures of the cat's face.

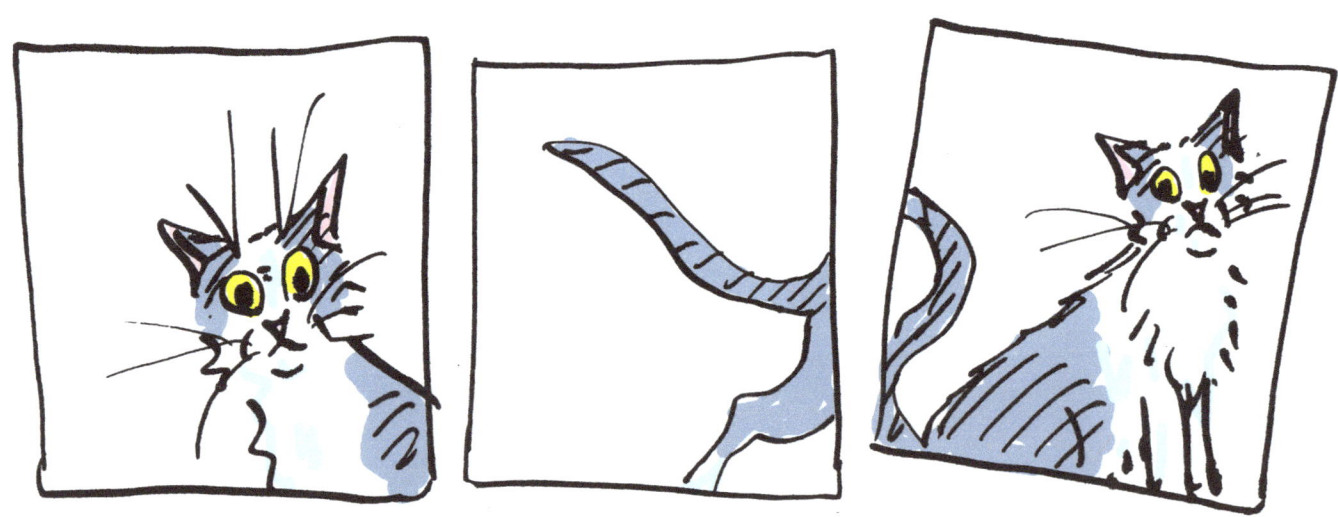

The sun was hot and Barney was cranky, so when Marci held him a bit too tightly, Barney tried to get away.

Poor Marci got **NINE** scratches from his sharp claws!

Barney didn't mean to hurt her; he was just scared and wanted to run. Marci had to go inside to wash up and put nine Band-Aids® on before any more pictures could be taken of Barney.

While Marci was inside, Michael took more pictures of Maggie. Michael was a special dog photographer so even though he didn't need any more photos of Maggie for the magazine, he took them for himself just because Maggie was so cute.

Michael had brought a red squeaky toy with him, and Shawna used it to get Maggie to look at the camera. Maggie wished she could play with the toy, but she never got to. At least she earned a **LOT** of treats, so she wasn't too sad.

By now **EVERYONE** was **HOT** and **TIRED**, but Michael needed pictures of Maggie, Marci, and Barney together. They moved to the shady part of the yard, and the three of them lay down on the cool grass.

At last Michael said he had only a few more shots to take, but they had to be on the window seat that Maggie and Barney often shared at naptime.

Oh dear, that meant they had to go inside the house…

…where Michael sneezed because of all the cats….

The window seat was upstairs in Marci's office. It was very crowded with Michael, Shawna, Marci, Maggie, Barney, and all the equipment all in there.

The equipment was set up quickly and Michael began rapidly taking pictures. Very soon he started sneezing and his eyes got all red and watery. Then he started **WHEEZING!**

"Excuse be, I thig I hab to go outside," Michael said in a choking sort of voice as he turned and ran out of the room.

After he left, Shawna packed up all the equipment and took it out to the car. When the car was loaded, Maggie, Barney, and Marci all stood in the driveway watching as Michael and Shawna drove away.

It had been a **VERY** long day and Michael had taken a **LOT** of pictures, over **2,000** of them!!

After Michael and Shawna left, Maggie, Barney, and Marci went inside and all lay down for naps in the cool house. It had been an exciting day and they were **EXHAUSTED!**

A couple of weeks after the photo-shoot, a small package arrived addressed to Maggie. Inside it was a beautiful flower made of red leather with a loop to slip over Maggie's collar! Shawna had made it especially for Maggie as a thank you for being so good. It wasn't a cookie, but Maggie wore it proudly from then on.

A few months later, right after New Year's Eve, the magazine came out! There were the pictures of Maggie, Barney, and Marci that Michael had taken, and there was the story of the magical moment when Maggie and Barney met.

Now they were **REALLY** famous because **10 MILLION PEOPLE** all around the world were reading their story.

Maggie and Barney weren't impressed since it didn't involve any more treats for either of them. They were just happy to be able to go upstairs and nap together on their window seat.

It really happened!

Marci really did get a call from *Guideposts* magazine about publishing the magical moment story from her book, **Maggie Adopts a Kitten (It really happened!)**. They sent Michael Brian, a celebrated dog photographer who was highly allergic to cats, to take the photos. The article entitled "The Cat Whisperer" appeared in the January 2012 issue. *Guideposts* had a circulation of over 10 million readers worldwide at that time. Here are some of the photos from that day.

Shaggy Maggie

Maggie's spiffy new haircut

Maggie performing on the table for treats

Michael Brian ©

Barney on the table, you can just see a bit of Marci's shadow as she holds him

Michael Brian ©

Maggie and Barney on the window seat

Guideposts story, January 2012

Lesson:

Are you allergic to something?

Some people are allergic to cats. Sometimes cats just make them sneeze, but they can still have them as pets. Michael was very allergic. Not only did he sneeze, but his eyes got red and watery, and he started having trouble breathing. He could not have a cat as a pet, but he wasn't allergic to dogs.

The special things about a cat that cause allergies are the saliva when he licks himself, his pee, and the tiny flakes of dry skin called dander that fall off all over the house. Sometimes brushing and bathing a cat will help lessen a person's allergies to it.

Some people are allergic to dogs, but only half as many as are allergic to cats.

There are lots of cats and dogs in the animal shelters near you. Maybe, if you aren't allergic, your family could adopt one or two of them.

Quiz:

1. What can happen if you are allergic to a cat or dog?
    a. You sneeze.
    b. Your eyes get red and watery.
    c. You have trouble breathing.
    d. All of the above.

2. If you are allergic to cats, are you allergic to dogs too?
    a. Yes.
    b. No.
    c. About half of the people allergic to cats are also allergic to dogs.

3. If you are allergic to cats, can you still have one as a pet?
    a. Probably not.
    b. Sometimes you can if the allergies are not too bad or you take allergy medicine.
    c. Maybe, if the cat is mostly outside or if you brush and bathe it.
    d. All of the above.

4. What happens at an animal shelter?
    a. Cats and dogs are kept in small cages.
    b. People can find cats and dogs to adopt.
    c. Both of the above.

Answers: d, c, d, c

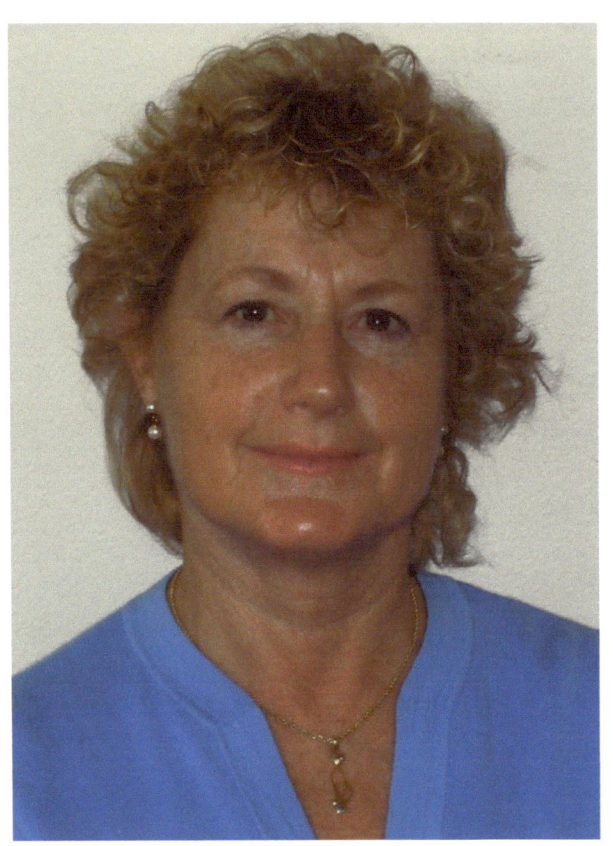

Marci Kladnik is an award-winning writer and photographer. She has won multiple MUSE Medallions and Certificates of Excellence from the Cat Writers' Association and was a finalist for a Maxwell from the Dog Writers Association of America. For seven years she wrote a newspaper column about feral cats while sitting on the board of Catalyst for Cats, Inc. Her work has been published in books and magazines, and she continues to write for various online and print publications. Marci served as president of the Cat Writers' Association for four years. She lives in the tiny town of Los Alamos, CA, with her dog and three cats.

Visit her website: www.maggiestories.com

Stephanie Piro is an award-winning cartoonist, illustrator, and designer. She is one of King Features' team of women cartoonists, "Six Chix," now in its 20th year of syndication. She has won multiple MUSE Medallions and Certificates of Excellence from the Cat Writers' Association and has been nominated for the National Cartoonists' Society's Reuben Award in the Single Panel Newspaper division for her single panel "Far Game." Stephanie lives in New Hampshire with her husband and three cats.

Visit her website: www.stephaniepiro.com

Michael Brian: "My opportunity as a photographer is a platform to raise global awareness of the magic dogs possess through visual imagery. I truly believe the animals of this earth are our teachers. They have a message to deliver, and I take it upon myself to be the messenger by creating images that are thought-provoking and compelling.

My influences over the years are too numerous to list, but it's the remarkable generosity of those around me that relentlessly push my evolution as an artist. My mentors are also integral components of my talented team. We are all of one mind and one spirit in our mission."

Visit his website: www.michaelbrianphoto.com

www.ingramcontent.com/pod-product-compliance
Lightning Source LLC
Chambersburg PA
CBHW041819080526

44587CB00005B/144